FOR WHAT IT'S WORTH

...

LOVE, DAD

BRUCE B SMITH

Author's Note:

While a child's head may be the hardest material known to man, a child's heart is as fragile as a hummingbird's wing. As a father I learned quickly that much of what I said or did could have a lasting effect on my children, for good or ill.

I also learned that sometimes saying nothing and just listening can be the wisest thing a dad can do.

In my career as a father, I've tried to be a good provider, teacher, photographer, repairman, radio controlled car mechanic, pine-box derby designer, fishing instructor, swimming instructor, and (God help me) driving instructor. I even took my daughter to buy her first prom dress (Note to all dads: don't *ever* do this!). I've changed diapers; bought, buried and prayed over several hamsters; and once in a while paddled a bottom or two (albeit reluctantly). And throughout the years I've never missed an opportunity to mumble, grumble, or occasionally whine about it all. But given the chance, I'd do it all again without hesitation.

It was, and still is, the most satisfying job I've ever had.

I won't pretend to have been the best dad in the world, but if I occasionally came close, the best mom in the world had me beat by a mile. Whatever I managed to do right I owe in large part to my wonderful wife and partner in parenting.

Some of the ideas expressed in this book were actual pearls of wisdom that I was lucky enough to come up with at the right time and in the right way. Others are things I wish I had said, or at least wish I had said better than I did back then. I'll leave it to you to figure out which are which.

I'll apologize now for the random organization of this book. It is, after all, a collection of thoughts and experiences garnered over the lifetimes of myself and my family. They're displayed here in no apparent order to you, the reader. But collectively, they represent some of the most treasured moments of a life well spent.

To My Kids...
For What It's Worth

No doubt you will remember a lot of the things you'll find in these pages. After all, you provided me with most of my material. Don't worry. Most of the really embarrassing stuff was left out, although I may decide to use it in a sequel. Chances are you will remember some of these stories a little differently than I do. And that's okay. It might be because I'm just a sentimental slob, or it could be the beginning stages of old-timer's disease. Who knows?

Some of these stories are my attempt to fill the vacuum created now that you've left home. And parts are my trying to put to rest my guilt over things I wish I had handled better. Others still will be those things I always meant to say to you, but never found the right time or opportunity. But most will just be a celebration of the life and times we've been lucky enough to share. You might consider treating this text as you do me: love the good parts, tolerate the not-so-good, and try to overlook the places where I miss the mark entirely by saying to yourself, "That's just Dad being…well, Dad."

Over the years I've tried to teach you everything I could. But it wasn't always easy to find the opportunity to pass along all of the lessons you'd need in life. So much of our time was lost with my being away at work. And what little time we were able to share was filled with soccer matches, tennis matches, crew races, ball games, scouting, and (God help me) puberty and dating. And then, all of a sudden…poof!

You were gone.

And there was so much more I wanted to tell

you…

How Did I Get Here?

Sitting here, I am painfully aware of just how much of a cliché I've become. You could accurately describe me as several gray hairs past middle-aged, warily viewing my midlife crisis through my Coke-bottle bifocals, lamenting my thinning hair and a growing paunch that often blocks my limited view of my large and rather unattractive feet.

In short, I'm a babe-magnet!

Actually, I think I may be morphing into one of those blue-haired pear-shaped people I used to laugh about. The only possible way I could be more ridiculous would be to buy a '70s muscle car and take up with a young bimbo. But one requires too much energy, and they both cost way too much money to maintain.

Not to mention, your mom would want to drive the car, and she'd expect the bimbo to help with the housecleaning.

But I can handle getting older. It's that other cliché that hurts the most, the one that describes me as an "empty-nester."

As I look around my home, I can see remnants of you kids everywhere. The house has weathered into a testimony of our time here, and the yard is landscaped with memories. With every day that passes now, I find I spend more of my time remembering our past, which leaves less time for envisioning the future.

Yes, all of you fledglings have long since flown. And to the untrained eye, it might appear that this nest is vacant. But I can assure you, any nest that has had you in it can never really be empty.

If you look carefully, under several coats of paint, you can still make out the pencil marks on the door frame in the kitchen where we measured your height from year to year. Each of you would stand your tallest, stretching your necks to gain that extra half inch. And Jen, you'd bemoan the unfairness of life as your younger brother Richard began to catch up.

Behind the garage is a small plot of land, where you guys used to help me garden, and where, later, we played baseball, horseshoes and badminton.

Over by the rock wall planter is where Richard's Cub Scout troop assembled scarecrows for a merit badge, and it was also there that we would place the arbor for Cathy's wedding.

In the grove behind the house I can show you where we built a clubhouse with a rope bridge and where you and friends had your race track set up to run your toy cars. The other day, I came across an unexploded paintball from a free-for-all you had when you were about fourteen. Apparently, paintballs aren't very biodegradable. .

Also in the grove was a dogwood tree that you used to climb. Sadly, the tree got diseased and had to come down. But the stump is still there. I can show you...

And there in the grove, not far from that dogwood stump, is where Jen eventually said her "I do's" with her new husband. And here in Cathy's room , which then became Jen's room and is now my office, I can still make out a few of Jen's damned self-adhesive glow-in-the-dark stars on the ceiling...I thought I'd gotten them all off, but they keep showing up. Wanna see...?

There in the enclosed porch is where you discovered that the dead bat you'd brought home wasn't dead, but just sleeping. And then you had to capture it before your grandmother came home. It was on that same porch where you first got a look at the German Shepherd puppy I brought home and you named him Champ.

I wasn't always this way. I mean, as much as you kids have been my life, I had another life before you came along. Back then I was Peter Pan, a loveable flake with no intention of ever growing up and certainly no plans for ever growing old. I was a kite, driven by the wind and in love with the exhilaration of it all. It didn't matter then that the winds sometimes dashed me to the ground. I'd pick myself up again and throw myself into the next gust, anxious for the thrill of the flight. Never worrying about where or how I might land next time. There were places to go and things to do and I was mid-stride in my step to take on the world.

And then I met the woman who would *become* my world.

I met your mom...

And somehow, looking into those green eyes of hers, I saw a future that I hadn't envisioned before.

Now, this book is not about my love life. (You kids couldn't handle it.) If it were, I'm sure you'd have found something else at the bookstore with a red-hot cover and a lot more pizzazz in it, something with a photograph of a bare-chested Adonis and tempestuous beauty with a significant chest of her own. But, in deference to your mom I feel obliged to digress for a moment here.

There have been countless descriptions of women penned by the men who loved them. And I am not so accomplished an author as to compete with the millennia of those artful phrases. Let's just say that all the things that have ever been written by men in love, about the women they loved, are all very true and accurate.

And they all describe my Deb.

I shudder to think where I might have ended up without her by my side. Remarkably, she never seriously tried to change who I was and let me remain my kite-like self. In fact, she has almost always celebrated my occasional flights of fancy. The only difference for me, now, was she held the string that guided me, and helped keep me aloft so I didn't come crashing to earth as much. And on those infrequent times when I did crash, she was always there to pick me, dust me off and launch me back into the sky. It's a rare woman who can do that for a man and continue to do it time and time again for a lifetime. I had, to quote yet another cliché, found my soul mate. But, she's more than that. Your mom *completes* me. She's the yin to my yang, the night to my day, and somehow she manages to accomplish all this and *still* be the pain in my neck.

She says much the same about me, by the way, but she describes her pain at a much lower point on the body.

Okay, so enough about that! The point is, I wasn't always "Dad." Like most dads, I started out as a kid. And like some of the luckier dads, I stayed a kid, at least on the inside, anyway. The problem I have now is that all *my* kids grew up and left me here with no one to play with anymore! (You ungrateful wretches.)

So it's up to me, I guess, to try to figure out: do I resurrect my Peter Pan self and coerce my wife into playing Wendy? Or do I accept the inevitable and do as so many men do...fading away into obscurity, spending my time in rocking chairs and gardening? Not much of a choice, really.

Yep...

Next stop, *third star from the left and straight on till* morning!

Something I Always Meant to Tell You:

The secret to a happy life is...

Choose something you love and dedicate your life to making it the best it can be.

I chose

you.

Something I Always Meant to Tell You:

Make decisions to better your life.

Everything else will fall into place more

easily.

Something I Always Meant to Tell You:

Remember that "better" and "more" are not always synonymous;

you need to understand what "better" means for you.

And what "more" will cost.

Something I Always Meant to Tell You:

Always stand on your principles.

It's one of your better characteristics.

Just try to be sure that you're really not standing on thin ice.

Something I Always Meant to Tell You:

When you're having a tough time
making a decision,

it usually means you already
know which choice is the correct
one.

You just don't like the
answer.

Home

The house sold a week before Christmas and our motley crew had piled into a car stuffed with pillows, blankets, a potty chair, and a nasty-tempered hamster. We were driving from California to Connecticut across the southernmost route along I-10 to I-95, a trip which would take us through several states over ten very cramped days. Richard was not quite three years old, and while initially excited about the trip, he began to lose enthusiasm when he realized this was not our typical afternoon drive. And as each mile passed, he grew even more miserable.

By day three of our journey a few things were becoming painfully obvious.

First rule of travel:

Rodents are not acceptable travelling companions.

That damned hamster was not only bad-tempered, he was a carnivorous little beast with a voracious appetite.

And his food of choice was Jennifer's fingers.

What had been Jen's adored pet was now for her a thing of terror, a blood-lusting little werehamster. I spotted the resemblance to Lon Chaney immediately.

Second rule of travel:

Potty chairs are not designed for mobile use.

As I repeatedly pointed out at the time, they're not called port-a-potties for a reason. Just try balancing the business end of a toddler on one of those pedestals at fifty-five miles per hour.

It was Christmas Eve in Terrell, Texas, when we discovered the third rule of travel.

Third rule of travel:

Never end up in Terrell, Texas, on Christmas Eve.

I'm sure the Terrellians love it there. After all, they *choose* to live there. But for a carload of road weary out-of-towners…it's best to keep driving.

We rolled into Terrell about dinner time to discover that the only eating establishment still open on this holiest of holy nights was the local convenience store. For our holiday fare, this shabby little predecessor to a 7-11 store offered up a dubious selection of cheap bologna and plasticized tiles of something called American cheese food. Any reasonable resemblance to actual food had been lost somewhere. These we laced with some soon-to-be outdated mustard on plain white bread and washed the whole thing down with canned sodas.

By then Richard had finally had enough. Tired, cramped and clinging precariously to that roller-coastering potty chair he began to wail. And in a tear stained voice, cried "I...wanna...go... *hooooooooome!*"

How could we explain to him that (for now at least), home was a 1981 Buick rolling along on Interstate 10? The home we had lived in since before he was born was now someone else's. Our new home was still several days and thousands of miles away, and still occupied by the soon-to-be previous owners. We would be staying with his mother's aunt and her obnoxious little dog for the next several weeks until the closing of the sale. Though the dog never actually bit anyone, the whole were-hamster experience had made me overly cautious.

Our answer (dripping with parental guilt and false bravado) was a very pitiful and unsatisfactory "We're going to our *new* home!" Because at three years old, Rich, you wouldn't have understood the answer I'm giving you now...

My son, it doesn't matter if you live in a castle, a condo, or a cardboard box.

Wherever you have family is home.

Your true home is made of the bricks of memories, and its foundation is cemented with the trust that you have in one another. Your true home is roofed by love that protects you when despair rains down. Home keeps you safe when the troubles of the world weigh heavy upon your shoulders.

Always remember, my son, that no matter how far you go, or how long you're away, *home* is always waiting for you—there, where your loved ones are.

And while buildings may get old and weaken, and possessions fade and lose their appeal, if you treasure the love of your family, *your home* will just keep getting stronger. At the end of your journey, it's the smiles of your family that say "Welcome Home."

That's what I'd tell you, if you were to ask me now…

But then I look at the young man you've become, and I think "*he already knows.*"

A Signpost for Jennifer

Your half-sister came to live with us when she was fourteen. Cathy was also my daughter, but by my prior marriage. And, as sometimes happens in families, we were struggling to sort through the remnants of love and resentments packed away in our emotional baggage.

It had been a particularly loud argument between me and Cathy, the ugly kind that parents and teens should never, but too often, have. And, gratefully, something you had never experienced before. After the shouting had subsided, you came to me with the wide-eyed wonderment only a six-year-old can summon so perfectly and said, "Daddy, I hope *we* never argue like that!"

I could have taken the easy way out. I could have used that particular opportunity to lay down some ground rules that may have ultimately been broken anyway.

But in one of those rare moments, the world froze…

My universe shrank to the space that surrounded me and you, my youngest daughter.

And I saw an opportunity…a chance to place a signpost in the road to help guide us later on. And I actually said the right thing (I think).

I looked down at your upturned face, your eyes reflecting a mixture of trust and concern, and, taking my best shot at parenting, said, "Jen, I'll let you in on a little secret. Right now your universe is pretty well made up of time you've spent with me and Mom and your grandparents. And for the most part, we usually have an answer for all the questions you can think up. So we must seem like we're pretty smart."

(Always the schmoozer, you nodded enthusiastically.)

"But someday, a few years from now, you'll ask about something and the answer we'll give is going to sound a *little* stupid. And for a while, the more things you ask about, the more stupid we're going to sound. And getting stupid answers will make you want to argue.

"When this happens, remember what I'm telling you now.

"It's not reasonable for Mom and me, and both of your grandparents, to suddenly get dumber, all at the same time. What will actually be happening then is that *you'll* be getting a little older and a little smarter. You'll question things more. And the simple answers we give won't be enough to satisfy you, anymore. So when this happens, let me know. And we'll work on providing better answers for you."

You looked at me for a second or two, nodding thoughtfully as you weighed what I said.

Then the moment passed, the world resumed spinning, and you ran off to play, leaving me standing there feeling somewhat foolish, but hopeful.

And life went on...

Some years later...I guess you were about twelve, interestingly not *quite* a teen yet, when out of the blue you surprised me by asking if I remembered that conversation so many years prior.

When I cautiously answered yes, you paused for a moment and looking up at me with that same six-year-old's innocence and wide-eyed wonder, exclaiming,

"Daddy! It's starting to happen!"

Look at me...Dad, the Oracle!

The signpost was still there where you and I had left it.

The road was clearly marked for us to proceed safely.

And, hand-in-hand, we continued walking down that path together; seeking smarter answers to the tougher questions you'd be asking of your stupid dad for years to come.

Something I Always Meant To Tell You:

To avoid going in circles,

always move toward something you want.

It's more productive than just getting away from something you don't want.

Parents Wanted:

Parents wanted to birth, nurture, and raise an unspecified number of offspring.

Birthing requires parents undergo a dramatic change of lifestyle, and abandon all prior concepts of freedom. Nights out on the town and impromptu partying will be discouraged. Prospective mothers will be expected to endure random periods of psychotic mood swings, cramping, nausea, prolonged vomiting, and labor pains: the equivalent of passing an eight pound bowling ball through one's rectum.

The prospective father will be required to comfort his spouse, ignoring potential danger of physical harm from said spouse's psychotic episodes. Random requests for ridiculous dietary urges are likely. Fathers will be expected to undergo frequent unscheduled verbal testing. Questions will consist of subtle variations of "Do you still love me, now that I'm fat?" Fathers must recognize that there is no correct response to any of these quizzes, and that any answer will likely be followed by the aforementioned psychotic episode.

Nurturing will involve an indeterminate number of feedings, burpings, and subsequent diaper changes which will occur on a schedule developed by the offspring. This schedule may also be changed at a moment's notice at the option of the offspring. During this phase, the father will be required to ignore the sudden plentitude of his spouse's bosom, as the increase in mammary magnitude is intended as a benefit for the offspring and not a bonus for Dad. Along with the breast swelling, aching and subsequent back pain, the mother will also endure endless leering by both offspring and spouse, though each is for distinctly different reasons.

Nurturing will also require frequent and prolonged sleep deprivation of both parents. As he or she grows, the offspring will develop new capabilities. Among these will be voice development, which typically begins as a gurgling noise, followed shortly thereafter by a lilting song-like crooning. This phase is notable for its endearing quality, and for the ear-splitting shrieks that immediately follow as the offspring tests his or her vocal range. Parental sleep loss occurs because this phase usually is nocturnal in nature and can last for several months.

Raising the offspring is an intensive exercise, requiring (but not limited to): teaching the child to walk, not walk, talk, what not to say in polite company, the meaning of the word "*no*," and how to stand in a corner and why...

When and where to urinate/defecate and expectorate; why there is air; why water falls from the sky; why ice melts; why the sun and moon come up and go down; how, when, and what to eat and drink; how to read; what to read; how and what to draw, color, and paint; how to clean all of this off the wall; the deluxe meaning of the word "*no*," and how to stand in a corner and why...

How to ride a bicycle, how to apply a bandage to the knee or elbow, the cold remedy benefits of Mom's chicken soup, how to drive an automobile, how to drive an automobile safely, what a "ticket" is, the ultimate meaning of the word "*no*," and what "grounded" means...

How to use a telephone; when to allow parents to use the phone; how to play Monopoly, baseball, tennis, and horseshoes; how to sled, snow ski, and water ski; how and what to cook; how to clean up a kitchen; how to make sure the clothes come out of the washer with same color and size they had went they went in; how and who to date; what a curfew is; and the absolute meaning of the word "*no*."

Successful parental candidates will need to maintain a separate full-time job to provide for their and the offspring's often extensive expenses, as parents will receive no monetary compensation for their efforts. Successful parents may enjoy a benefit package that includes love, gratitude, and fond memories. However, there are no benefits guaranteed. This position is a lifetime commitment that cannot be terminated...ever.

No experience necessary.

OFFSPRING

WANTED:

Wanted: An unspecified number of male and/or female offspring to assist would-be parents in creating a loving family.

The candidate child should exhibit characteristics of trust, determination, bravery, understanding, and love, as the prospective parents have no prior experience in child rearing and are therefore likely to make many mistakes.

The child will undergo rigorous potty-training and receive a conventional education including advanced life skills, as well as training in social interaction and language skills, with emphasis on the words "yes," "no," and "maybe." Candidates may expect to experience frequent hugs, kisses, cuddling, and tickling. Occasional spankings are possible.

The candidate mother shows excellent potential as a nurturer and role model. She is sensitive, intuitive, educated, perceptive, understanding, giving, dedicated to motherhood, determined, and wise beyond her years.

The candidate mother comes with a grandparent bonus package offering numerous opportunities to be spoiled rotten.

The candidate father has a good heart, tries hard and may do okay...eventually.

Compensation will include free room and board, weekly allowance with incentive bonuses, 100% medical and dental care package, full education including college tuition assistance, Christmas bonus package, birthday bonus package including cake of your choice, liberal taxi services, and a lifetime of unlimited love.

Successful candidates need only apply. There is no interview.

Something I Always Meant to Tell You:

Making another person's decision for them is as dangerous as it is futile.

Illuminate their choices, but always let them do the choosing.

Something I Always Meant To Tell You:

Life is a series of trade-offs.

You never gain something
without leaving something
(or someone) behind.

Be certain the value
of your gain is worth
more than your loss.

Trading Up

watched your face as you gazed longingly at the object of your affection. The two of you had been through a lot together. And it was obvious that this was a serious relationship. Our view was from the rear, and while more flattering, it really accented her oversized spare tire.

Personally, I preferred trucks. But you'd always been a Jeep guy, and this little buggy had taken you through the Connecticut hills for a good many years and had always gotten you home safely. You and the Jeep had navigated through some tough times, and more than once the two of you had gotten jammed up on a rock or a stump. But ultimately, the two of you together were unbeatable.

But times change, and as you both grew older, I knew it was the memory of that relationship that held you together. Your futures were diverting onto separate trails and the parting would be a hard one for you to bear. Harder still would be letting go of the freedom those four oversized knobby tires represented.

While a man can have several things in life he loves, there can only be one love of your life. And you were wrestling with the dynamic forces of the universe in trying to maintain two. A choice had to be made and it was clear to me that the time for that choice had come. But it was yours to make and I was just there for moral support.

You could continue investing every spare cent into keeping that Jeep running...or say goodbye to the past, sell the Jeep, and use the proceeds to buy an engagement ring for Lynn. For a Jeep lover, not an easy decision to make.

The Jeep was your freedom, an always-available opportunity to escape adulthood and run off to play in the woods.

Lynn, of course, had been a part of your life for some time now. But the relationship had hit the point where, if it was to survive, a stronger commitment was called for. That commitment required saying a final goodbye to childhood abandon, and hello to being a husband and maybe, someday, a father.

We both knew, of course, what the correct answer was. But it was you who needed to voice it. I could only stand by as you grappled with your indecision.

Finally, I succumbed to that fundamental parental need to provide, if not guidance, then clarity. And I asked you,

"Can you imagine your life without Lynn in it?"
'Nuff said....

So the Jeep is now a fond memory and Lynn is officially your fiancée.

And life goes on.

Something I Always Meant to Tell You:

There are two things you'll own in this life that are worth more than all the rest of the world's treasures combined.

One isn't really yours, but you'll earn it just the same. And with luck and hard work, you'll keep it.

The other is yours and yours alone. It's something you earn for yourself every day of your life. And if you ever lose it, it's almost impossible to get back.

The first is another person's trust.

The second is your integrity.

Something I Always Meant to Tell You:

If it were easy,

Anyone could do it.

Something I Always Meant to Tell You:

Witness the drowning man:

A fellow who never learned to
swim. See how he thrashes about in
a panic, screaming for help?

If only he could keep his wits, he'd
probably discover that the water
isn't more than hip-deep.

A lot of life's problems
are like that.

Something I Always Meant to Tell You:

Always remember:

It's your life.

It's the only one you get.

So enjoy it.

Something I Always Meant to Tell You:

Commitment is a virtue,

not a sentence.

You're always
free to change
your mind.

Something I Always Meant to Tell You:

Most bridges don't need to be burned,

just crossed.

Something I Always Meant to Tell You:

Love...completely.

Trust...wholeheartedly.

But do both selectively.

Something I Always Meant to Tell You:

Wisdom comes from experience.

Experience comes from trying...and failing.

If you never fail, you're probably not trying often enough.

Something I Always Meant to Tell You:

Pride comes from successful
accomplishments.

Balance your pride with humility,
though.

After all, your
accomplishments
are in the past...

It's what you
do today that
counts. (See
Wisdom)

Relationships
(and the art of plumbing)

The bathroom sink must be the most over-utilized and under-appreciated altar in our house. I mean, the entire family pays homage there daily, conducting our individual rites in the blessed privacy provided by the all-imposing bathroom door.

Poised over its porcelain finish and shiny chrome faucets, we brush, floss, comb, pluck, primp, and flex our muscles in the mirror (not *me*, of course), secure in the sanctity of our relationship with this bastion of personal hygiene and civilized life.

And yet, as any man will testify, it is the most hell-ish thing on earth to try and repair. With the never ending cycle of family members washing God knows what down that drain, it just has to get plugged up from time to time.

Now, (forgive me ladies) but women are no help here. My wife was adept at managing the most disgusting mess in a diaper, but would be thoroughly gagged by a few gobs of hair in an otherwise innocent drain. It's some gender specific thing, I think.

Once that drain is plugged and the altar is unavailable to the worshipping masses, it's usually Dad that goes to work.

That would be me, of course.

But I first have to empty the cabinet under said sink.

In there is a Smithsonian-sized collection of forgotten bottles of shampoo, hair conditioners, hand creams, unmentionable personal paper products, and hundreds of nondescript little vials of unimaginable concoctions for hair care, skin care, nail care, and some things I really don't care to talk about in mixed company.

Then I commence phase two, which involves squeezing my manly self into a cabinet that isn't much larger than the typical litter-box. Come to think of it, our last litter box had a larger opening. Please note here that the cabinet is always suspended a sadistic three inches off the floor, causing one's back to bend at a painfully unnatural angle. Thankfully, the emptying process usually yields two or three half-empty tubes of muscle rub to be used later on.

I was lying under the sink one day, wedged half-in and half-out of that little cabinet, trying to determine how much of my swearing vocabulary I would have to use before the *$#@ pipes stopped *$#@ leaking. I find swearing has a calming effect on me and absolutely terrorizes the plumbing.

Maybe it was the fumes from all the *$#@ products, but all of the sudden it hit me...

Relationships are like your bathroom sink.

Really, if you think about it for a second or two, it has an almost Zen-like logic.

The two people in a relationship are like the hot and cold faucets in the sink. Turn them both on (metaphorically speaking here), and they'll blend to make things warm and comfortable.

As long as each faucet (person) is allowed to flow freely, then water (life) will move along just fine.

But if one faucet gets bound up, then things will get too hot or too cold. And that's just not good for any relationship.

And if they're both bound up, nothing flows, things get stagnant and the relationship dries up.

Work with me here...

Even a pair of good flowing faucets (people) will eventually accumulate a little debris (issues) in their pipes.

It's not a big thing and usually easily fixed.

But if you've got a lot of things stored up under that cabinet, (like bottled up resentments?) you're going to have to clear them away first.

Then you can get back to flowing like good faucets... I mean *people* should.

(Like I said, it might have been the fumes.)

Dad's Ideas about Working

Unless you hit the lottery, invent something marvelous, or inherit millions from some relative I don't know about, you *are* going to have to work for a living. (I'm sorry.)

Decide what "successful" means to you and work to that end. Never buy into someone else's idea of success.

Work to live, never live to work.

Make a list of your dreams, your goals and what you value most in life. From time to time, pull out your list and see how you're doing. Revise it as you go along. But keep the original list intact. To see where you're going, it sometimes helps to remember where you've been.

When you find that friends and family are interfering with your work, you've lost your priorities, and it's time to take the family on a vacation. Remember: work to live, not the other way around.

Getting more money for a job you don't like is a trap to be avoided. Once you have the money, your expenses increase and you're stuck where you are.

Your employer rents your time and talent. Make sure you give him value comparable to what he's paying. But remember, it's a rental, not a lease. Tomorrow is never guaranteed.

Almost everyone eventually tries to climb the management ladder. Middle management can be that rung where you're held back by the people above you and weighed down by those below you. It's a rung that can be very hard to hold onto. But remember, succeeding at supervision requires you to enforce your boss's values as if they were yours. And it's easy to get the two confused after a while. The happiest people are often found at the top and even the bottom rungs.

Unless you're a CEO, supervision will usually reduce the value of your time monetarily. Even though you're paid a higher salary, you will always be expected to put in more effort and time than you're compensated for. This doesn't mean that supervision is necessarily a bad thing. In fact, you might actually enjoy it. If you happen to be a CEO though, please remember your good old dad and send me a check every now and then.

Going...Going...

From the first day you entered our lives, our days and nights were spent around you. Here you were, this little person-in-the-raw. Perfect in the eyes of God (and those of your parents), but needing all the training required for a life on your own...someday.

We taught you to read, to write, to walk, and (against my better judgment) to talk. We answered 3,877,463 questions that started with the word "why." We played with you, and tickled you at every opportunity, delighting in your cackles and screams. We showed you how to build a fort in the backyard if the weather was good, and a tent in the living room on days when it rained.

And if you cried, we'd hold you until you felt better. We bandaged scraped knees and elbows. There were countless trips to the emergency room for various injuries and ailments. We worried over you, and about you. And always, we loved you.

We smiled bravely for your benefit, while choking back our tears, as we watched you leave for your first day of school. And then we set aside time in the evening to help you through those rougher patches of homework. And often scrambled to keep up with all you were learning.

We taught you to ride a bike and watched you ride away...out of our reach and beyond our little circle of safety. Later on, we taught you to drive a car, and watched the clock when you were out with friends, always praying that you would soon be home safely.

Over the years we sang "Happy Birthday to You" so many times... and wrapped (and unwrapped) probably hundreds of Christmas presents. How many Easter eggs got colored over those years? And on Halloween it always seemed to rain.

We starved (as the mosquitoes feasted), while your baseball games crawled through those final innings. And we applauded and preened at your graduation and I was an embarrassment (as always) with my camera.

And we tried not to cry as we helped you pack your belongings before you left for college. And I was always amazed at how Richard left with one duffel bag and a basketball, while Jennifer required my fully loaded pick-up truck (twice).

For almost two decades we devoted our lives to preparing you for the time when you would eventually leave to be out on your own...

How ironic it is that no one prepared us for the time when you'd actually be gone.

A Girl's Night Out

I t's a nice dream, one of my favorites. I'm lying on a beach somewhere, soaking in the sun, sipping on one of those frozen drinks that have the little pink umbrellas in them. The drink is being served up by a lovely native girl who wears a beautifully white smile and not much else. Crystal blue waves are caressing the shore as I listen to the distant calls of the seagulls...and the bells. (Bells?)

Ring-Ring!

As any parent will testify, a telephone ringing in the middle of the night is never a good thing. No one ever calls you with great news after midnight. I mean, has anyone ever been notified that they've actually won something at twelve-thirty a.m.? Does your great-uncle call to say he's decided to make you his only heir in the wee hours?

Uh-uh.

Ring!

My wife is well aware of this, too. So the cowardly woman handed *me* the phone.

"Mr. Smith? This Mrs. C...I hate to bother you so late, but...is my son there?"

Young master C was Cathy's boyfriend. It was a relationship I wasn't too thrilled about. How many fathers can warm to a black-leather jacketed kid who drives a van? Confused and still half asleep I might have been, but I knew for certain that her son wasn't hiding under my bed or anything, and I mumbled something to that effect.

"Well," she continued. "Is your daughter Cathy there?"

"Of course." I responded, "She's asleep in her room."

As all good *children should be.*

Obviously, Mrs. C's son was *not* in that category.

"Could you check to be sure?"

(*The nerve!*)

Now, I knew Cathy was asleep. As a matter of fact, she was so tired she turned in early. I mean, how many fifteen-year-olds complain of being so tired that they go to bed at nine o'clock?

(*Ding!*)

Now I was awake.

Peering quietly into her room, it was obvious Cathy was in her bed, hunkered down under the blankets. Tip-toeing a few steps closer, it was even more obvious that I'd been snookered by one of the oldest tricks in the book. There was no innocent daughter under those covers, just a couple of poorly arranged pillows. Also, the window was wide open with the screen removed.

And standing next to her bedside was this pitiful example of an unsuspecting and somewhat oblivious father...

(that would be me).

There were a number of courses for me to take at this point.

I could call the police.

Let's not get too carried away, just yet.

I could jump in the car and hunt the little delinquents down, dragging my errant offspring home by the hair of her empty head.

We're not supposed to be getting carried away, remember?

But after surveying her room, I concluded that she hasn't taken any of her belongings with her, including her purse and house keys. So it was likely this was a rendezvous and not an elopement. Neither alternative was desirable, but it did alter my level of response.

By now, my outrage was cooling and my veins were filling with the icy calm of a father with a plan. I advised Mrs. C that it all likelihood they would both be home before morning, which was only a few hours away. We agreed to get in contact with each other if the kids weren't back by seven a.m.

After hanging up the phone I returned to Cathy's room to consider my next course of action. Mumbling a silent prayer for guidance, I straightened her blankets, gently putting her pillows back where they belonged. Tenderly, I reached out across her bed and...

...locked her bedroom window, shut off the lights and went back to bed.

It was an hour or so later that I thought I heard the distant rumble of Mr. C's traveling bordello driving away. A few minutes passed as I held my breath and waited.

There was a period of silence as I imagined Cathy coming back to her window to make her re-entry. Several more minutes passed as she discovered the locked window and considered her options. By now, young master C had departed (and cell phones weren't invented yet), so her options were few, if any.

And then I heard her tentative steps on the graveled walkway that passed beneath my bedroom window and lead to the back porch. Then came the quiet jiggle of the back door handle (locked, of course) and then more silence.

I could have gotten up at that point and confronted her. She was expecting that, I think. But a confrontation would just feed an argument, which would drive a wedge even further into our tenuous relationship. Something more subtle was called for.

It was late spring, not yet warm enough to be comfortable, but not so cold as to be a danger of frostbite, either. There was a lounge on the back porch and I knew where she'd be in the morning, so I drifted off to catch another hour or two of sleep.

My alarm went off at five a.m., and I made my way to the kitchen to make some coffee. Outside the kitchen window, Cathy lay asleep on the lounge. She was curled up in a fetal position, and it had obviously not been a warm and cozy night. No doubt her dreams had been of the comfortable bed that lay just on the other side of her locked window.

I had made a pretense of ignoring her until now. But she stirred and then saw me. As I poured my coffee she came to the window and asked, "Can I come in?"

I looked at her for a very long time, considering my response. She and I both knew that the message she deserved had been delivered quite effectively.

I met her at the door and answered with two carefully chosen words. "This time."

And that was it. Well, not really. She was grounded, of course. And there would be other "discussions" and confrontations. Eventually, Cathy graduated from high school. Remarkably, this was accomplished without my killing her, or her giving me a heart attack.

Somehow we managed to survive it all and actually hammer out a relationship of love and mutual respect.

We didn't speak of that night for many years. And, to my limited knowledge, she never again skipped out for a night on the town. Now, twenty years later, Cathy and I laughingly refer to those tempestuous teen times, and she tells friends the tale of her "Girl's Night Out."

Nightmare

I t was the Friday before Columbus Day, and Jen was looking forward to a long holiday weekend. She had finished her only class for the day, and was driving down from her school in Vermont to meet her boyfriend at the University of Connecticut.

It was raining heavily as Jen turned left on a busy highway. The left turn light changed from yellow to red just as she was making her turn. The man in the pickup truck approaching rapidly from the other direction saw his now green light and pressed his accelerator.

The truck was traveling at over fifty miles per hour, and the driver didn't see Jen until it was too late.

There was no time to hit his brakes. Still accelerating, the truck struck the passenger side of her compact car, crushing the rear and side passenger compartments around the driver's seat.

The only area of the car's interior that remained intact was where Jennifer sat. Exploding glass from the passenger door became shrapnel that embedded deeply in Jen's head, arm, and hand. The impact of the collision whip-sawed her head between the driver's door and the collapsing windshield, as the truck continued like a juggernaut, propelling her car over forty feet, before finally allowing it to come to rest up on the curb.

She sat there, semiconscious, as people came running to help.

***

The telephone rang as I walked in the door. It had been a particularly rough day at work and traffic on I-95 had moved at a crawl due to tons of holiday traffic and the heavy rains. I really was not in a mood to take yet another message from one of my children's friends. They always seemed to call when Jen and Rich weren't home.

I picked up the receiver and heard "Mr. Smith? This is Nurse so-and-so from Hartford Hospital." My wife's an Emergency Department manager, so my first thought was this was a message for her, not the kids.

I must have misunderstood something and I asked her to repeat it. "Mr. Smith, your daughter, Jennifer has been in an automobile accident and she's being treated in our trauma center."

The world stopped.

Somehow the whole world slipped out of focus, and yet, irrelevant little details remained crystal clear. The clock on the wall, the colored magnets holding the kids' photos on the fridge,

Jen's picture is there

the cupboard door I'd left half open that morning.

Somewhere in the distance the nurse was still talking. I responded with mechanical assurance that I was on my way, while I tried to remember what highway exit to take for the hospital. Ominously, all the nurse would say was that Jen was awake and was able to give them our phone number.

How do I tell her mother?

Looking back now, some of the details of that day have gotten lost. My wife tells me I called her at work. But I can't tell you what I said. I know I tried not to alarm her, or to betray how terrified I was. I remember snippets of the drive to Hartford. My white knuckles on the steering wheel, the rain and the endless squeaking of the windshield wipers are remarkably clear memories. Reaching across the seat, I took my wife's hand as the exit signs passed by the window so slowly...much too slowly.

As we walked into the Emergency Room they were just wheeling Jen out on a gurney to conduct a CAT-scan. I think I took my first full breath when I saw she was alive. And then I realized her beautiful mane of hair was matted to her scalp with blood.

How could there be so much blood?

Her right arm and hand had been injured, apparently by the car window as the glass shattered on impact. I was overcome by the physical need to touch her, to hold her. I needed to transfuse her with some of my own life force. I took her uninjured hand for a few brief moments, as her mother and I assured her everything would be okay. She grasped my hand in return and tried to persuade us not to worry. She seemed so small, lying there. Jen was short, to be sure, but you wouldn't describe her as petite. Petite suggested frailty, and Jen could never be considered frail.

Until now.

While we waited what seemed endless hours, we called her grandparents and our son, Richard, giving them what little information we had.

I know we spoke to a doctor that night. He was a trauma surgeon and by reputation, a good one. But again, I don't remember his name, or what he looked like...just an endless maze of corridors leading to his office, and what he had to say. Most of his diagnosis was in med-speak and lost on me, though my wife seemed to understand fully.

I only remember the reverberation of certain words. Jen had suffered a severe concussion and probably experienced brain damage. They'd know more after the scan and some other tests. They would keep her at least overnight to monitor her condition. We should prepare ourselves for the likelihood that she would not be returning to school, not this semester and possibly not ever.

This can't be happening. Not to my little girl.

From the time she took her first steps, Jen was always a force to be reckoned with, intelligent, funny, and determined to excel. Always tiny, she made up for her size by tackling life head-on. With Jen it had always been lead, follow or get out of her way. As a coxswain, she demanded the best from the rowers on her crew team. She was talented, too, and had won awards in computer graphics, painting, drawing, and sculpture. She thrived on challenges in academics and had graduated high school third in her class. Now a college student, she was carving out a niche for herself in wildlife biology.

Until now.

Choking back our fear and apprehension, my wife and I entered Jen's hospital room. The extent of the injuries to her brain couldn't be fully assessed until the swelling from the concussion subsided. Though she smiled and tried to reassure us, my heart was breaking for her.

For me, it wasn't my college-aged daughter lying in that bed, but the toddler I had tickled so many years before. It was the little girl I had taken for her first hairdresser appointment, and the tousled-haired tyke who'd held my hand as I tucked her in at night.

They say that when you face death your whole life passes before your eyes. Tonight it was my daughter's life that was passing before me, and it was tearing me apart. This child that God had given my wife and I, this child we had raised and taught and nurtured and protected for all of these years, was, in an instant changed in ways we couldn't imagine, and that we were powerless to prevent.

We held her for a time and then to reduce her fears and apprehension (*or ours?*), we laughingly tried to make light of the situation. In an effort to do something productive, we set about getting her comfortable in her room for the night. We busied ourselves getting her settled in and chatted about the quality of care she'd received, trying to create some semblance of our normal relationship. And prayed that life would once again be normal.

Jen's hand gingerly probed her scalp as she looked confused and said "My head hurts." Chillingly, her next sentence brought us back to reality. "Where am I?" she asked.

My wife shot me an apprehensive glance and I felt my knees turn to jelly. "You're in the hospital," she carefully replied.

Jen puzzled over this for a second, looked at her mother, and asked, "Why?"

Jennifer had been in the hospital since late that afternoon, and it was now past ten at night. Yet, she didn't know where she was or why. She remembered leaving school that day and stopping for lunch. However, beyond that, the day was a complete blank. She couldn't remember why she left school or where she was going. She didn't remember the half-ton pickup truck that careened into her driver-side door, exploding the door glass and collapsing the door, pinning her in the car. She didn't remember the Samaritans who pleaded with her to hold on as the ambulance sped to the scene or the paramedics who strapped her head to a board so they could extract her from the wreckage. The hours of being probed, swabbed, x-rayed, and bandaged hadn't happened for her, and never would.

When we tried to explain what had happened, we discovered she could only retain what we said for a minute or two. And then she'd ask again, "Where am I?" and "What happened to me?"

Patiently we'd repeat our answers, more slowly each time, and each time she'd consider our answers for a second, but her brain kept misplacing the information. She needed some baseline to build on, and her mind couldn't provide one. She was stuck in an endless cycle of erase, reset, and rewind.

I was swept away by another wave of fear as we realized Jen couldn't grasp the simple concept of the nurse's call button at her bedside and was genuinely confused and completely mystified by the nurse's disembodied voice responding over the intercom. With each terrifying moment that passed, we were discovering the horrible extent of her injuries.

But there would be no resolution for her condition this night. Plus, she was beginning to show signs of fatigue and needed to rest. Though we were tempted to do a bedside vigil throughout the night, the best therapy for her now was a good night's sleep. In the morning we would begin the frightening task of determining the full extent of her injuries. As we had so many times before, we held her for a short time, then tucked her in and kissed her goodnight, leaving her with the promise we'd be there for her in the morning.

Later that night, my wife and I held each other and cried as we shared our fears about our daughter's condition, and her future, both the one she had before the accident and the drastically different one she now faced. In the end, we were just grateful she had survived and would help her in any way we could. And we prayed.

The next day we brought our daughter home. The doctors had decided there was no need to keep Jen hospitalized. Ironically, although her brain had sustained a dramatic impact, her other injuries were not life threatening. What damage had been done could be treated only by months of therapy and understanding. The next weeks would be spent discovering the full extent of what we would come to accept as her disabilities. Which of these were permanent and which would pass was a mystery that only time would resolve.

Some of her challenges were oddly comical. She'd answer the phone and congenially talk at length with whoever called. But when she hung up, the call (for her) had never happened. This became a comic opera of missed phone messages for everyone.

The most endearing change was Jennifer, herself. The girl we brought home from the hospital was not Jen the college student, but Jen the ten-year-old daughter we'd known and loved so many years before. She was innocent and trusting of everyone in a puppy-like fashion. She didn't bear the fingerprint of experience that adulthood brings. This Jen was happy to snuggle up under my arm and watch a movie or doze, where the normal Jen might have loved to do that, if she only had time for it. We'd talk openly about the differences in the hope that it would ultimately help her regain herself. She'd ask questions about what she was like before, and she was disdainful of her prior self. It became routine for her to refer to her pre-accident self as "Evil Jen."

For the most part, though, Jennifer's limitations were formidable and frightening. For instance, Jen couldn't interpret messages from her own body. We would have to remind her to eat because she couldn't recognize the sensation of hunger, and could only complain that she felt "strange."

My daughter, who began writing words at age three and had routinely made the Dean's list at college, suddenly couldn't read. She'd recognize the words, but couldn't comprehend their meanings. It was the same for her with writing. She'd know what she wanted to write, but halfway into the sentence, the thought would vanish.

But two things had not changed. While not the overachiever she once was, Jen still would not accept limitations on herself. And though her memory had suffered a crushing blow, her fighting spirit was still intact. She was determined to recover, complete her schooling, and go on with her life.

Jen would not return to school, however, for many months. She would need several tests to assess the level of her injury, and therapy sessions to retrain her brain to process information and retain it. Somewhere in those months of trial and error, Jen began to make headway. Her accomplishments were achieved in baby steps and gradually gained momentum. She'd use mental tricks to improve her memory. She would write notes to herself to help her remember.—and then, almost comically, forget where she put the notes.

Her mother and I were there through it all, just as we were when she learned to ride her first bike.

We helped her along when she needed it, and forced ourselves to stand back and let her do things on her own when we thought she could. And we kept our tears—and fears—for the times when Jen wasn't around to see them.

Remarkably, over the next year, Jennifer recovered almost fully from her injuries. But term papers that used to fly off her pen now took considerable hours of trial and frustration. Concepts that she once grasped naturally involved much more thought and concentration. But, true to her nature, Jen either overcame or learned to work with all of the obstacles she had been presented with and went on to live her life on her own terms.

The young woman we had sent to college was competent, self-assured, sometimes intolerant, and fiercely independent. The little girl that came home with us from the hospital was more understanding, vulnerable, and trusting. In a way, the accident allowed us to reconnect for a while with the child we had raised so many years before. In a bizarre sense, I'll always be grateful for that time.

And when anyone asks, I tell them as horrible as it was to endure, the hardest moment for me wasn't racing to the hospital that day, or when we were looking down at her battered body on that gurney. No, the hardest moment for me came over a year later when she had healed enough to return her classes at college. When I truly understood how fragile our lives really are, and still I had to let her go.

Richard and Dad Go Fishing (and Richard Learns some new words)

My son (bless his heart) has always been eager to join me for just about any of my well-intentioned, but sometimes misguided, endeavors. He does these things with me because he loves his dad and with the full and complete knowledge that, in all likelihood, his dad doesn't have an ice cube's chance in hell of doing *anything* simply. This is a long-standing tradition that I've honored and he's endured since his earliest years and it all began with fishing.

Our first father and son fishing trip required the loan of my in-laws' boat. Gert and Bill had used the first three letters of their names and christened their little lake boat the *Gerbil.* Cute, huh? My firm belief is that they got that three letter sequence backwards. The *Gerbil* would have been more appropriately called the *Bilger,* as it seemed to be forever destined (through no fault of its own) to do its very best impersonation of a submarine. To be fair, it was a sturdy little fourteen-foot tri-hull and very stable, the perfect family boat. Its propensity for taking on water was most often due to operator error (that would be me).

At the insistence of my mother-in-law and against his better judgment, Bill agreed to let me take command of the *Gerbil* for a father and son fishing expedition. My wife could barely contain her pleasure at the prospect of Richard and me sharing some quality time together. It would be a good experience for us manly men to bond over a can of soda and a bucket of worms, and if we were lucky, we might actually catch something other than a cold. The bonus here was that Deb then got to enjoy a day of relative peace and quiet, as the two biggest troublemakers in her life would be out in the *Gerbil,* out on the lake, and out of her way. Richard, of course, was a virtual whirlwind of excitement. He was going fishing with his *Dad*! Just the two of them! At four years old, he had never been fishing, of course. But if *Dad* liked it, it must be really cool!

Curiously, no one ever questioned my boating experience.

I mean, when a guy takes his four-year-old son out onto a body of water that's more than six inches deep there should be some fundamental issues addressed.

One, can you swim? (*A bit. Does dog paddling count?*)

Two, have you ever driven a power boat before? (*Well, no...but I did once own an inflatable raft. It sank on its maiden voyage.*)

And three, do you have enough life jackets?

Actually, had anyone asked about these things or dared to question my experience, I would have lied through my teeth. In fact, after three decades of fatherhood I can proudly say that I've become accomplished at a good many things, not the least of which is lying about the things I know absolutely nothing about. It's a defense mechanism and all my wife's fault, really. She is infinitely more mechanically inclined than I am, sinks basketballs (with nothing but net), and understands the principles that govern the known universe on par with Einstein. I've had to become adept at lying about almost anything just to keep up. Let's just say that when I'm in the midst a repair of any sort, the phrase "Dad, is this *really* going to work this time?" is a virtual mantra in my home.

That being said, Richard was in safe and competent hands for his first fishing trip (*not!*).

But first, we had to get prepared. Those uninitiated in the ways of us fishermen would think you simply get the boat in the water and commence catching fish. Ha! Little do you landlubbers know, but there is a *process* to any successful fishing trip.

The first step of this involves untangling the orgy of hooks, lures, bobbers, sinkers, leaders (and

Band-Aids), left in the tackle box from the last fishing trip. It is one of my favorite theories that the manufacturers of these devices go so far in designing a life-like lure that, once the box is closed and away from prying eyes, the little buggers actually try to mate. It's the only reasonable explanation for the obscene arrangements they get themselves into.

Next, you have to unsnarl the spaghetti factory that was left on your reel from the last trip. Take my advice: do this out of earshot of any children. There are some phrases they probably aren't ready to hear just yet.

It's always appropriate at this time to also discard any half-eaten sandwiches you may encounter in the bottom of the tackle box, although with the amount of preservatives present in the average slice of bologna, it may be possible to survive on these morsels years after they've been prepared.

Next, you have to gather up some bait. Now in the old days, when I was a lad, back when men were men and women were women and dinosaurs roamed the earth, we'd go out in the yard and dig up some worms. Not today. Nowadays we know that what entices a discriminating native American bass or trout is a fresh, juicy Canadian night crawler. Not only are they six times the size of your average garden worm, bearing a striking resemblance to a small python, but let's face it, they're *imported.* And how often does an American fish get a chance to eat a Canadian worm? It's gotta be a major attraction, right? Not to mention there's no digging required. You buy them from your local bait shop in a convenient little cardboard container like they use for Chinese take-out. (Which relates to another of my theories on the mysteries of Chinese food and why lo-mein looks the way it does.)

Now you're good to go. With bait, tackle box, rods and reels, and lunch, dutifully prepared by Mom, you're finally ready for adventure. And so it was Richard and I set out for our first father and son fishing trip.

All in all, things were going well and according to plan. It took three and a half hours to get ready to go fishing that day. I probably spent another twenty minutes hooking up the boat trailer to the truck and checking the trailer lights, etc. And it took all of ninety seconds to trailer the boat down the hill and across the street to the boat launch. Did I mention we live next to a lake?

It would take me another ninety seconds to nearly sink the boat and almost drown my son, and I would accomplish all this in three feet of water, twenty feet from shore.

That's probably a little over dramatic, even for me. Let me explain. I *really* love to fish. And, after days and weeks of anticipation...after hours upon hours of preparation...I was in sight of my goal. The fish were out there calling to me. The water was there, the boat was there, and Richard and I were there. At moments like this, I look at the most efficient method of getting the ball rolling, so to speak. In this case, I had a boat to put in the water. I had all sorts of fishing tackle to put in the boat. I also had a four-year-old son to put in the boat. This, of course could all be accomplished by putting the tackle and the son in the boat and then putting the boat in the water.

Efficient?

Yes.

Simple?

Definitely.

Smart?

Not very…

My enthusiasm was contagious and Richard was as excited as I was as he danced around on the deck, elated. But his expression began to lose some of its enthusiasm as I winched the boat off the trailer and it began slipping into the water. Standing at the bow, his face shifted from euphoria to apprehension as he began to perceive his situation. Something between horror and the resignation of a condemned man crossed his face as the rope played out and the boat floated freely from the trailer. As he drifted farther and farther from shore it probably occurred to him that on previous occasions when he had done something wrong and I'd threatened to kill him, I might have actually been serious.

Anxious to get started, I unfastened the winch cable from the boat and began to rewind the winch. The boat, which was still floating freely by the way, was starting to drift further from shore.

"Dad?"

"Yeah, Son."

"Dad, there's some water in the boat."

In the back of the boat, in what I had learned was called the "stern," was the "bilge."

(I love those nautical terms, don't you?)

There was always a little water in the bilge, though I could never figure out why. But the boat never seemed to mind, so neither did I. Not bothering to look up, I kept winding that winch (a heck of a lot of line for such a little boat, I thought), and I told Rich not to worry, everything was okay.

Soon we'd be out there on the lake hooking more trout and bass than any man has a right to dream of. The women would be proud of us. My father-in-law would beam. We'd all be dining on fish for a week and we'd never ever have to worry about going hungry. Everyone would rave about the humongous bass Dad and Rich had caught. And I, of course, being an experienced cook, would develop new and tantalizing recipes for preparing fresh fish. I'd write a best-selling cookbook. There'd be television appearances...

(It's amazing, really, the stuff that goes through my head.)

"Dad?" (a little higher pitch to his voice).

"Yes, Rich?" (still cranking...).

"There's a *lot* of water in the boat!"

It was at this point that a small bell started ringing somewhere in the back of my brain. And in midcrank, I looked up.

Imagine if you will, a pint-sized miniature of the Titanic. The *Gerbil*, my father-in-law's flagship, appeared to be attempting a swan dive in reverse. The lake had somehow risen to within an inch or so of the top of the boat at the stern. The Creature from the Black Lagoon was rising from the depths to climb aboard and attack my child. On closer inspection, I realized the just-visible creature's head was, in fact, my parting glimpse of the boat's outboard motor as it dropped below the surface. The bow was frantically pointing skyward, trying to indicate to the sinking stern what the direction of choice should be in this situation.

And standing at the bow, clutching the bow's rail in one tiny hand and a life cushion in his other, was my son, only four years old, and doomed to be the reluctant captain of a ship headed for Davy Jones' Locker. He stared at me in horror, the whites of his eyes growing from the size of baseballs to truck rims as he realized for an instant that Daddy might just be trying to kill him, after all.

I tried not to swear in front of my son. He was very impressionable and tended to do whatever I did. So I tried, really, to set a good example. But at moments like this nothing t works as well as a few good swears. And, before I could stop them, the words erupted out of my mouth,

"*Shit! Godammit!*

Hearing this, Richard knew he was in serious trouble, and the whites of his eyes grew even larger.

Pause with me here for a moment, please. I have, in very short order, gone from (a) anticipation, to (b) determination, to (c) exhilaration, and now (d), which stands for desperation.

Is it any wonder so many dads end up as manic/depressives? Gone are the accolades from screaming fans for my rave seafood recipes, replaced by a screaming lynch mob of a wife/mother and grandparents as I try to explain how I lost my father-in-law's boat, and, incidentally, drowned our son ninety seconds from our house in three feet of water!

I stopped cranking the winch and grabbed for the *Gerbil's* bowline.

Pause with me here again.

As you review this text, you'll find that at no previous point do I make *any* reference to the bowline. Ideally, back when the boat began inching down the trailer en route to what would be its watery grave... it's at that point a *reasonably* intelligent person would secure the bowline so the boat couldn't drift away. Right?

Unfortunately, all reasonably intelligent people were busy elsewhere at that moment, and Richard was stuck with...me.

Not to worry, though. Everything is under control. As the boat sank another inch below the surface, I yelled to Richard to throw Daddy the bowline!

One more pause...

How many four-year-olds do you know who have the slightest clue as to what a goddamn bowline actually is?

I thought so.

The rope, Richard! The rope!

Richard, always anxious to help, especially when his life is at stake, dutifully grabbed the bowline and dropped it over the side of the boat, a full twenty feet from where I stood.

In a final act of desperation, I waded out in the three feet of water and, as it happens, the two feet of silt (there is some really smelly stuff in the bottom of that lake), and carried my son to shore. Placing him safely on the ground, I trudged back, retrieved the bowline and winched the boat back up on the trailer.

Now, if saving a boat from sinking is a noble thing, then saving a four-year-old from drowning should elevate one to hero status.

Right?

Well, I mean, if you forget how it all almost happened and all...

Right?

Exactly!

Which is why I wasn't going to mention this to anybody at all, least of all Richard's mother. After an hour or two of fishing, Richard would forget all about our Poseidon adventure, and no one would have to know.

And I was right!

We pumped out the boat and found the drain plug laying in the bottom of the bilge. Apparently, *someone* had removed it while cleaning the boat and *someone* had forgotten to put it back. (You'll never prove it was me!) After an hour or two of fishing, in which time we caught innumerable sunfish but no bass, I brought my exhausted little boy home. The boat was back safely; my son was back, equally safely. We endured the "lousy fisherman" jokes from the family, and no one was any wiser.

Until later...

My wife and I were watching TV when my daughter Cathy came in and asked in an incredulous tone if we had any idea what Richard was doing. We acknowledged that we did, as his mom had just put him in the bathtub to soak the smell of all of those sunfish out of his skin.

"I know he's in the tub," Cathy said. "But do you know what he's *saying*?"

Peeking around the bathroom door, the three of us watched as Richard, my sweet little fishing buddy, took his toy boat and drove it around the surface of the bath water.

Bbbbbrrrrrr... Bbbbrrrrr

I felt a rush of parental warmth come over me as I realized my son, bless him, was reliving the joy of our fishing trip!

Bbbbrrrr...and then he stopped, pushed the boat underwater, cackled with glee, and yelled one word: "shitgoddammit!"

Then he plucked the boat off the bottom of the tub, drained it out and repeated the whole performance again.

And each and every "shitgoddammit!" would provoke peals of laughter from him...and from the three of us hiding behind the door. My wife glared at me with that familiar "Is there something you're not telling me?" look.

(Busted)

Faced with the irrefutable evidence and a living eyewitness,

(Maybe I should have killed him, after all.)

I was forced to confess. I endured the slings and arrows of derisive laughter and ridicule. And I still do, every time the family gets together to rehash old memories. Let's face it, this is the kind of material wives live for. But we men…we testosterone types… we know what's really important. Richard and I faced adversity and survived to tell the tale!

Now, you'll have to excuse me, my son is coming over to take me fishing.

But I think I'll wait on the shore while he unloads the boat.

Just in case…

Halloween

Holidays are the exclamation points that emphasize the otherwise routine days of our lives. There are holidays like New Year's Eve and New Year's Day that mark old endings and new beginnings. And, of course, Christmas, when our children share their joy and wonder with us, and in that sharing recharge the spirit of the child that still lives within us. Holidays can be marvelous memory makers. And then there's Halloween.

You just can't make an eloquent statement about the nobility of man at Halloween. It doesn't inspire people to do charitable acts or to bestow blessings on anyone. Quite the contrary! Halloween is for pranksters and tricksters and for scaring the bejeepers out of any unfortunate soul who happens to let his guard down. And, despite numerous protests and murderous threats from my wife, that's the tradition I've always tried to uphold in my family.

Now, in order to effect a truly notable Halloween memory, you need a few very basic ingredients:

pumpkin

dark night (preferably with a spooky moon)

imaginative child (add more as desired)

shameless and sadistic father

It's long been the tradition in my family that Dad and the kids go hunting for "The Perfect Pumpkin." Come to think of it, my wife *never* does this stuff. Makes you wonder who thinks up these traditions, doesn't it? What the heck does she do with all that free time while I have the kids out scouring the markets for pumpkins and such? To be fair, though my wife certainly enjoyed those periods of temporary peace and quiet, the kids and I always had a great time and, while Mom's acquisitions would be affected by budget constraints, Dad's purchases never had a limit. Where Halloween was concerned, there was no price too high for the perfect pumpkin! This was a tradition that I used for virtually every holiday, by the way. Hence, the perfect valentine, the perfect Christmas tree, etc. But I digress.

So the kids and I would set out in search of the "Perfect Pumpkin." This was always a description and title that was subject to some interpretation. Each of the kids would find what they felt constituted "perfect" and there'd be an impromptu judging contest. We'd oh-so-seriously examine the characteristics of each gourd, trying to visualize how the poor thing was going to look after we hacked out its insides and carved some ferocious countenance on it. Eventually we'd reach a consensus and hightail it back to the house with our prized, and soon to be butchered, "Perfect Pumpkin" in hand.

The autumn sun was sinking rapidly behind the hills beyond our home as the kids and I set about drawing pumpkin faces on scraps of paper. After several attempts at a number of designs, we agreed upon the face that would scowl down from our living room window at the hapless trick-or-treaters who dared come to our front door. We copied the features from our drawing to the pumpkin and I selected the largest butcher knife from the kitchen to do the deed. With my eyes bulging as best I could, I gave my best impression of Boris Karloff and, screaming for just the right effect, plunged the knife into the gourd! This was, of course, met with a round of applause from the kids and a smile and shake of the head from my wife. After completing the incision for the unfortunate pumpkin's craniotomy, we'd commence scooping its "brains" out. (Always good for a *yechhh* or two.). Finally, all that remained was to put the candle inside the head and place our jack-o'-lantern in the front window. By this time, the "traditional' side of me was in full swing and I suggested that Richard go out front to make sure the pumpkin could be seen from the road.

Now, I'm really not a bad father, *usually.*

But it was Halloween and tradition demanded a sacrifice. This year, Richard drew the short straw, so to speak. Richard, of course, was ignorant of my adolescent adherence to arcane family rituals. He was only six, going on seven. By now he knew there was no Santa Claus, but chose to believe anyway, just in case. And at this moment, he knew there was nothing outside that could hurt him, (but what if he's wrong?). His sister (the shark) smelled blood in the water and insisted she'd watch him through the window to make sure he's okay, and he reluctantly agreed to go. This was as much a testimony to his gullibility as to her cold-bloodedness.

By now, the sun had long since left the horizon and it was pitch-black outside. Timing is everything with traditions, you know. And Richard, fearful but trusting Richard, made his way slowly, step-by-cautious-step, down the back stairs and around the corner of the house (where the shrubs and trees take on monstrous shapes and it's *really* dark), and finally to the front curb to gaze upon the pumpkin as his wonderful, loving father, whom Richard adores, suggested.

My son was no sooner out the door and cautiously heading down the stairs, when I made a bee-line for the drawer where I kept *It*!

It was a full head, rubber mask that looked, at its best, like a demented old man. At its worst, *It* was a demented old man that lived to eat the flesh off the bones of six-year-old boys. *It* had craggy brows over dark, deep set eyes and a shock of platinum white hair that rose like a scream from the fringe of its balding top. And *It* was going to meet Richard on the path back to the house. Realizing the benefits of special effects and good lighting, I grabbed a flashlight on my way out the door.

By now, Richard had made it to the curb, given a cursory glance to the front window, just to say he did it, and confirmed that, yes, the pumpkin is visible from the road. And now he was headed back to the safety and security that waited for him inside his well-lit house, just past the trees and beyond the dark and forbidding back yard. And there, in the backyard, *It* waited. Richard, either sensing the danger or anxious to be back inside, was moving much faster now. Gone was all caution as he rounded the corner of the house. Running at full clip, he broke into the clearing at the back of the house and headed toward the stairs.

Suddenly, *It* jumped out of the bushes. *Aaarrrgggghhhh!*

And Richard screamed...*aaaaaiiiieeeeeeeee!*

To get the proper effect, I held the lit flashlight under my chin so as to cast shadows across the mask and make it more menacing. I needn't have bothered, really.

Completely frozen in place, Richard was still screaming...

By then, I was behaving like a merciless mirthful ass, virtually collapsing with laughter, and then I realized...

Richard was *still* screaming, and I was about to be in serious trouble!

Quickly, I removed the mask and shone the flashlight on my face so Richard could clearly see me, but he kept screaming! And I heard his mother coming...

Hearing his terror, my wife had become a she-bear, bursting through the backdoor to save her cub...

Downstairs, the grandparents have heard the commotion and come running...

His sister, sensing a change in the atmosphere, is no longer the shark and is now only concerned for her brother's welfare... (The little traitor!)

Guardedly, I looked into his mother's eyes, and suddenly, I knew what real fear was...

With his mother's appearance, Richard's screams have finally subsided into an incoherent muddle of sobs and gibberish, as his mother attempted to keep him from going into shock or something worse.

Meanwhile, there I was, holding a flashlight and a scary mask, trying to look innocent and not doing a very good job of it.

Eventually, Richard calmed down, and being extremely goodhearted, he forgave me.

His mother however, was not quite so goodhearted, and certainly not as forgiving.

But by the time the Halloween had passed and that rotten smelly pumpkin had been disposed of, we were once again a happy, reasonably well-adjusted family.

Finally, October was just a memory, Thanksgiving came and went.

And then the kids and I set out to find "The Perfect Christmas Tree."

The Perfect Tree

There's magic in the first year of a marriage. It's a time of sharing, of learning about each other's good points and some of the bad one's too. It's a time for living in the "now," and dreaming about the future. And so it was for me and Deb.

We had been married for not quite a year. And we certainly had the magic. She was working at her job and in her last year of college, while I was working at the other end of town and attending night school forty miles away. Our tiny one bedroom apartment was sparsely furnished with a dining set her folks had given us as a wedding present and an old bed and dresser. When we were lucky enough to both be home at the same time, we'd curl up together in the old, beat-up, but conveniently oversized, beanbag chair that made up our living room furniture.

Magical!

Frustratingly, our school and work schedules never coincided, and we'd often go a day or two without really seeing much of each other, so we would leave notes of love and encouragement to each other instead. After a while, we acquired a tape recorder, and we'd record impassioned and often humorous messages that we'd laugh about later.

Magical!

And one of the most precious memories I have of that time is our first Christmas.

In a year of sacrificing and saving, of building and planning, Christmas was the most magical time of all. Like most newlyweds, we had very little money for decorations and our tree was a scrawny little thing with a few gangly limbs and not very tall. But it was beautiful! It stood proudly in the corner of the living room, surrounded by a carpet of pine needles that kept falling off prematurely. We had managed the expense of a few cheap ornaments and tinsel. It was simultaneously pitiful and absolutely glorious. Amid the dime store bulbs hung a single ornament, not matching any of the others, with the year "1977" boldly emblazoned on it, and, in smaller letters, **"Our first Christmas Together"** written below the date.

I can't remember what I bought Deb for Christmas that year, or, for that matter, what she got me. But I remember that tree. And I remember that ornament. Christmas passed, followed by New Year's Eve and the tree, its needles now almost totally gone, made its way to the curb to be carried away by the trash collector. Our tawdry little collection of bulbs and that dated ornament were packed away and forgotten...until the next Christmas.

Of course, we had accomplished a few things in that second year. Deb had graduated from college. I had finished with the trade school and had a new job in my chosen profession, at a firm closer to home. Home had changed too, as we moved up to a two-bedroom apartment. The second bedroom served as additional storage for the stuff we seemed to be collecting almost daily. The bean bag was still there and we still used it regularly. But we now had a sofa and chairs for guests should any drop by.

And, suddenly, it was Christmas again.

I was in the card shop looking for "Just the Right Card" for Deb. You know the card, the most beautiful one on the shelf, the one that says in a few choice words, all the things you ever wanted to say, and for less than $1.95? That's the one. After looking in two other shops and searching through endless racks of cards dripping with prose and sentimental goo, I found "Just the Right Card," paid the lady behind the counter (considerably more than $1.95, as I recall), and was walking out the door when I saw it. Over on the shelf, next to the decorative bulbs, but off to the side a bit to make it stand out...and it said "1978," and, below that, **"Christmas Together."** And so the tradition continued.

That Christmas, we decorated our tree, a little larger this time, and, after watching a collection of romantic holiday shows, Deb looked lovingly at me and said "Let's make a family." And we did. (Who was I to argue?)

And like clockwork, Jennifer arrived nine months later. By the time the tree was up that year, we had moved into our first house, Jennifer was a few months old, and we still had our first two dated ornaments, plus three new ones (two were gifts) that said "1979 – **Baby's First Christmas.**"

(Readers should note here that I now switch this narrative from "romantic reminiscing" to "frantic father" mode. I can't help it. It just happens every time my kids get involved.)

Somehow, it evolved that I was the designated dated ornament hunter. Each year, I would set out to find the dated ornament that aptly expressed the most significant event of that year. Oh, for the days of only having to find "Just the Right Card" again. "Baby's First Christmas" was again a no-brainer the year Richard was born. Then there were ornaments commemorating Grandma and Grandpa. I went a little nuts for a few years and got dated ornaments with Santa in a hot air balloon, Santa in a fire engine, Santa on a motorcycle, Santa on a bicycle, etc. There's a Mother Goose ornament (the wings actually move), and ornaments with raccoons and penguins and one or two with kittens, (to commemorate our cats). There are fairies and elves and even a moose, thanks to Jen's (temporary) passion for them.

And it became a tradition each year, for the kids and I to venture out in search of "Just the Right Tree." As our collection of ornaments grew each year, so did our trees. And each year, I would provide endless rounds of laughter and entertainment as I tried to trim the tree at top and/or bottom to make it fit in its customary corner in the living room. This always involved a series of adjustments in height with varying degrees of success. One year I trimmed a little too zealously, and we had to set the tree on a white sheet to conceal the cement blocks underneath. Other trees couldn't find their center of gravity and would have to be wired to the wall and the fireplace mantle.

But each year I did somehow manage to get "Just the Right Tree," and everyone would "ooh" and "aah" appropriately. Then Deb would sit on the floor, passing the various decorations out to the kids. Each child, in turn, would seek out the ornament that meant the most to them. And then they would lovingly attach it to a conspicuous spot on the tree and back to Mom quickly to get another.

Magical!

Eventually, finding "Just the Right Ornament" to represent the significance of the year became a quest of momentous proportions. My family, with their varied interests and issues, didn't make it any easier. By Christmas of 2000, I was at my wits' end. Jennifer was going to Australia that year to do a semester abroad. It would be the first Christmas away from home for her. For my little tribe this was a big event! Now imagine trying to find an Australian Christmas tree ornament. Now try finding one in New England! Keep trying. You see, the Australians don't seem to have Christmas trees! At least not the ones in Tasmania, which is where she was headed.

But if nothing else, I am versatile. Which, I suppose, is why these tasks often land in my lap. Being modestly talented, I commenced carving the 2000 ornament out of balsa wood. After several fiascos, I managed a passable kangaroo, with 2000 emblazoned across its tummy and a girl wearing an Aussie hat popping out of the pouch. If you really scrunch your eyes up, in a darkened room, after a cocktail or two, you might say the girl bears a fleeting resemblance to Jennifer. But, from my viewpoint, it's worthy of Michelangelo.

After the Aussie ornament came a fireman's hat for Richard, who entered college that year to become a fireman. And then a likeness of Deb's dad, Bill, riding on his beloved Craftsman lawn mower. He'd be mowing the north forty in heaven about now, I guess. Next, I'll be making wedding bells with Jen and her husband Phil's pictures inside. And then, maybe one of my mother in-law, doing her crossword puzzles…

Now when I look at our Christmas tree and I see all those ornaments that mark the many milestones of my family's life, I get a little teary-eyed. The dreams and tears and fears and accomplishments of all the years are chronicled there for each of us to see and to share. I wonder how many ornaments there will be when my children take their children out to find their tree.

I've never seen a less than perfect sunset or sunrise. A Christmas tree is like that. Each one is different, and yet, each is perfect in its own way. I've come to learn that the perfect tree is literally, *any* tree that we choose to grace our home. What makes it unique—what makes it *perfect*—is that we gather as a family to share our memories, our dreams of the future, and our love for each other.

But rest assured, this December I'll be out in the snow and sleet and rain, searching through slush and mud, looking for that Perfect Tree. After all, it's a tradition.

Bedtime

All my bags are packed, I'm ready to
go
I'm standing here outside your door
Hate to wake you up to say goodbye
But the dawn is breakin', it's early
morn
The taxi's waiting, he's blowin' his
horn
Already I'm so lonesome I could cry.

So kiss me and smile for me
Tell me that you'll wait for me
Hold me like you'll never let me go.
I'm leavin' on a jet plane
I don't know when I'll be back again
Oh, babe, I hate to go.

- Peter, Paul & Mary

There is a lifetime of memories stored up when you raise children. If you're lucky, as I have been, most of them are pretty nice. Among my favorites are those I've collected over the years around bedtime.

Every night, after dinner, and homework, after the TV shows and bath times, Mom would usually play the warden and announce it was time for bed. Sometimes this was met with pleas to finish a TV show or a board game that was almost won, or lost. Ultimately though, the children knew they couldn't get a reprieve on their sentence and they, pink cheeked, pj'd, and smelling freshly of soap, would shower us with hugs and kisses and then toddle off agreeably to their rooms.

But while a reprieve wasn't in the cards, a stay of execution was always available because Dad got to tuck them in. This process was guaranteed to last a considerable length of time. First, there would be a last minute news update on the biggest event of their day. This was usually explained to me amidst beaming smiles and excited whispers so as not to provoke the Warden's attention. The Warden would inevitably pop in at some point to remind me in a ruefully good-natured way, "Bruce! You're as bad as the kids!" and that I was supposed to be getting the children ready for bed, not inciting them to riot. This too, was part of the ritual of our evening, and accepted by all as part of the process.

Next would come the prayers. "Now I lay me down to sleep…" with ample blessing for Mommy and Daddy and Grandma and Grandpa and Smoky, the hamster, and Boots, our cat, and our dog, Coco, or Champ, a later dog, or Kao, (you guessed it, another dog).. And finally, I'd tuck them in, collecting more kisses and hugs along the way. And then I'd head for the door and shut off the light, say goodnight one more time and hear the last request of the day. Sometimes, they'd ask me to read them a story. But usually it was, "Daddy, can you sing us a song?"

There are a vast number of memorable vocalists in the world. And compared to Pavarotti, Neil Diamond or even Jon Bon Jovi, my singing voice would probably rank about tenth...behind Lassie.

But for those few precious moments, I was a star. And my audience was a select group of V.I.P.s with exclusive seating to a sold out concert for that night only. How could I treat it as anything else? So with the bedside lamp as my spotlight, I'd sing. Sometimes it would be songs my mother had sung to me like "Old Shep," or "Bobby McGee," or some other ballad that fit the moment. As fate would have it, my job at that time sometimes required me to travel, and often these trips would keep me away from home for several days at a time. Like so many dads, I hated to go, but it was my job. And it's those times I remember most. On the night before I had to leave, Jen would always ask for Peter, Paul, and Mary. And I'd sing:

"All my bags are packed, I'm ready to go..." Sometimes, she'd chime in, harmonizing, "leeee-avin' on a jet plane..."

Afterwards, we'd hug one more time, with more kisses , and I'd exit quietly, stage left. Nowadays, I try to remain philosophical about those precious moments I missed traveling away from home. And I realize it's those "special" moments, when our time is limited, that makes our lives and our memories all the more precious.

Recently, Deb and I visited Jen and our son in-law, Phil, who now live thousands of miles from here.

The night before our flight was scheduled to leave, I looked at Jen and began quietly singing,

"All my bags are packed... I'm ready to go..."

Quickly she clutched my arm and said,

"Please don't, Dad. You'll make me cry!"

Guess I still got that old star quality, huh?

Something I Always Meant to Tell You:

Most people really want to be nice,

,but sometimes you have to give them an opportunity.

Some people may need several opportunities.

Something I Always Meant to Tell You:

You are the writer and star of an implausible (and sometimes impossible) soap opera titled

"Your Life."

And each day you'll write and improvise your way through another episode.

Now:

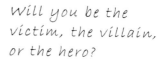

Will you be the victim, the villain, or the hero?

P.S.

You may be the star, but not every episode will be about you.

Something I Always Meant to Tell You:

Free advice is always readily available.

And it's often worth every cent you've paid.

Even when it's from me.

For What It's Worth...

Though we had a lifetime to talk about, we didn't know how to begin. Finally, I said goodbye, hugged him, and walked out of the room knowing that, in all likelihood, I'd never see him again. This man I called "Dad" was dying of liver cancer. It would happen quickly. And all the words that needed to be said would never pass our lips. All of the harbored guilt and explanations and recriminations (and the love),

all of that would remain here on earth…

with me.

"For what it's worth" implies that there may be some level of value present. In this text, it is up to you to determine what value, if any, can be found here. These stories may strike a chord with parents or their children, or they might not. If someone reading these words pauses to say, "I've been there!" then I've accomplished part of my goal. If my children can read this and laugh (or cry a bit perhaps), then I've accomplished another part of my goal.

For what it's worth, I didn't start out to be a father, or an author, for that matter. In the beginning, I was just busy being...well, me. However, after my father died, I discovered the devastating weight of the burden I was carrying in all those things that Dad and I'd left unsaid. And I realized that God had shown me an opportunity to change that legacy handed down from my grandfather, to my father and then to me. I had a chance to break that chain of silence and leave my family with something more... something that could be shared, free of regret or obligation. Something that frees us all from that "things I should have said while I had the chance" garbage. And if this book achieves that...well, then I've accomplished all of my goals.

For what it's worth, I've had a remarkable life. I've loved and been loved. There's been good times and not so good times. But, all in all, I can't complain. And, when the man upstairs decides (someday) that it's time for me to check-out...I'll have the last laugh. 'Cause then, after years of quests for the perfect tree, the perfect card, ornament, pumpkin, etc., someone else will have to go find "The Perfect Head Stone."

For What It's Worth

Love,

Dad

CPSIA information can be obtained at www.ICGtesting.com
Printed in the USA
LVOW101522120612

285785LV00010B/10/P